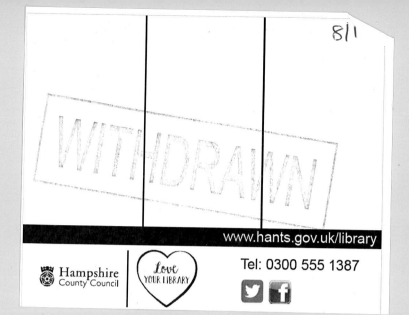

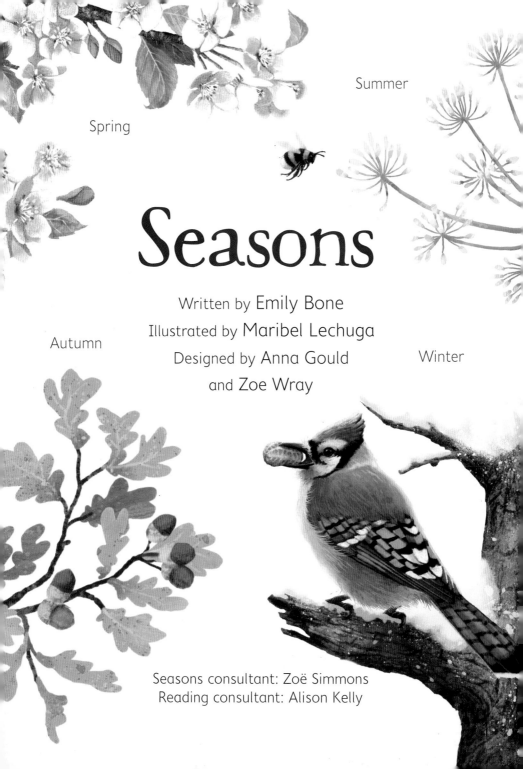

Spring

Summer

Seasons

Written by Emily Bone
Illustrated by Maribel Lechuga
Designed by Anna Gould
and Zoe Wray

Autumn

Winter

Seasons consultant: Zoë Simmons
Reading consultant: Alison Kelly

It's spring. There is lots of rain
followed by warm sunshine.
This makes flowers grow.

Tulip

Daffodil

Crocus

3

Some trees and bushes grow
flowers too. Birds eat the flowers.

Cedar waxwing

Forsythia

House
finch

Red
maple

Apple

Northern cardinal

5

Birds build nests in the spring.

Swans pile up twigs and reeds to make a nest at the side of a river.

The mother swan lays eggs. She sits on them to keep them warm.

Babies hatch out of the eggs.

Baby swans are
called cygnets.

The cygnets follow
their parents into
the river.

7

Many animals have babies.

Deer have babies called fawns.

Wolf babies are called pups.
They're born in underground dens.

Frogs lay hundreds of eggs.

Frog eggs are
called frogspawn.

Tadpoles grow
inside the eggs.

They hatch out and grow into frogs.

9

In summer, it becomes much warmer.
Summer flowers grow.

Bees, butterflies and other
bugs feed from the flowers.

Marjoram

Fennel

Ox-eye daisy

Bumble bee

Hoverfly

Monarch
butterfly

Black-eyed Susan

Chafer
beetle

11

Butterflies lay eggs on plants in the summer.

Small white butterfly

Egg

A caterpillar hatches out of the egg. It eats the leaves.

Caterpillar

Birds catch caterpillars.

Blue tits

They feed the caterpillars
to their chicks.

Trees grow leaves and the
grass grows long in summer.

Animals eat the trees and grass.

Sheep

Rabbits

Harvest mice live
in long grass.

They weave the grass
into round nests.

Summer nights are warm.
Some creatures are awake.

Hawkmoths feed
from flowers.

Other moths look
for partners.

Silk moths

Giant leopard moth

Agave flowers only open at night.
Bats feed from them.

Agave
flower

Mexican
long-nosed bats

Badgers hunt for worms and
beetles to eat.

As summer changes to autumn,
fruits and nuts become ready to eat.

Apple

Blackberry

Rose hips
grow from
rose flowers.

Acorns grow
on oak trees.

Some drop to the
ground. Animals
eat them.

Wild boar

Some animals collect food that
they will eat during the winter.

Acorn woodpeckers make
holes in trees to store nuts.

Squirrels bury nuts under the ground.

Black bears eat fruits and nuts during the autumn. They won't need to eat for the whole of winter.

Mountain ash berries

The weather starts to cool down.
The leaves on trees turn red,
orange, yellow and brown.

The wind blows.
Leaves flutter off
the trees.

Maple leaf

22

Ash leaf

They settle on
the ground.

23

It gets colder later in the autumn.

Swallows fly away
to places that have
warmer weather.

They gather in big
groups before they go.

Other animals try to stay warm.

Hedgehogs make warm nests in leaves.
They sleep in the nests all winter.

Peacock butterflies find warm places
such as sheds to rest.

It gets very, very cold in the winter. Plants die and many trees have no leaves.

White tailed deer

Sometimes it snows. Snow settles on the cold ground.

There isn't much for animals to eat. Some birds eat food that they collected during the autumn.

Blue jay

Peanut

Animals have ways to keep warm.

Birds fluff out their feathers and huddle together.

Bluebirds

Mice dig tunnels under the snow where it's warmer.

Owls hunt for mice hiding under the snow. A great grey owl hears a mouse moving.

It swoops down into the snow.

It uses its sharp claws to grab the mouse.

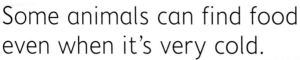

Some animals can find food
even when it's very cold.

Bison use their noses to push
snow out of the way. They eat
the grass underneath.

Holly trees grow berries in late autumn. Birds eat them during winter.

Thrush

Holly

Deer eat fruit, nuts and grass during summer. In winter, they eat twigs and moss instead.

Roe deer

At the end of winter, plants begin to grow again. Snowdrops are one of the first flowers to grow.

Snowdrops

Digital retouching by John Russell

First published in 2017 by Usborne Publishing Ltd., Usborne House, 83-85 Saffron Hill, London EC1N 8RT England. www.usborne.com Copyright © 2017 Usborne Publishing Ltd. The name Usborne and the devices ♀⊕ are Trade Marks of Usborne Publishing Ltd.